Know Your Worth

Love the Skin You're In

By Charlotte Flood-Walls

Know Your Worth
Love the Skin You're In

This is a book of poems that relate to women of color who have triumphed over probabilities we face daily in your communities. The poems reflect our trials and tribulations that we have overcome at some point in our lives. We are not all born with the confidence portrayed in this book, however for the ones who have displayed this level of confidence, they can reflect upon us. These poems show us how to love ourselves, believe in ourselves and focus on the word of God, who instills love in us. We were created in God's image to shine brighter than the stars in the sky, that's no lie. Genesis 1:27 Philippians 2:15

We are so many shades of Beauty and sometimes we can't see it no matter how hard we look because our society makes us think and feel otherwise. This contributes to our low self-esteem. We must uplift and encourage each other as strong young girls and women using the influences of the ones before and around us that have defeated these insecurities. This will help us recognize who we really are and how we really look to everyone else and ourselves, which is simply self-worth. Upon the completion of reading these poems that were straight from my own experiences as a young girl into womanhood, I pray you will know you are exquisite. Rather, it should be that of your inner self, the unfading beauty of a gentle and quiet spirit, which is of great worth in God's sight. 1 Peter 3:5

To conclude, I want all the shades of colorful women to be inspired knowing that we are beautiful inside and out. Love yourselves and know that you are loved. When you look in the mirror say to yourself, "I love me, and God loves me". Do not let any unwholesome talk come out of your mouth, but only what is helpful for building others up according to their needs, that it may benefit those who listen. Ephesians 4:29.

Dedication

To all my sisters young and old whom the world may have made feel inadequate.

You were the seal of perfection, full of wisdom and perfect in beauty. Ezekiel 28:12

For you created my inmost being, you knit me together in my mother's womb. I praise you because I am fearfully and wonderfully made; your works are wonderful; I know that full well. Psalm 139 13-14

Poems

Self-Worth 7

I Love Me 8

I Will Not 9

Loving Me 10

Proud 11

Self-Esteem High 13

Precious Gem 15

Beauty 17

Blessed 19

Dark Skin 20

Many Shades 21

I Am 22

Royal Love 23

Enough 24

Black Girls 26

They Say 28

My Color 29

Black Queen 30

Queen 31

Skin Tone 32

In Love with Me 33

Thick Brown Hair 34

My Grin 35

Respect 36

Creativity 37

I Validate Me 38

Mother 39

Black Love 40

Girl of Color 41

Know Your Worth 43

Know Your Worth

Love the Skin You're In

By Charlotte Flood-Walls

Illustrated by Mildred Kathy Flood

Self-Worth

The ebony in our skin keeps the beauty within, and that smile on the outside no need to defend,

Hips curvaceously aligned with our shoulders to perfection,
Our eyes beautiful & brown no reflection,

Lips plump, sweet as passion fruit on the vine,
I don't know about you, but my God made me just Fine!

Ezekiel 28:12 NIV

I Love Me

I Love Me, I love me first, not second

I love Me, I love my hair thick; naturally Curly, not straightened

I love Me, I love my Ebony Skin, not Ivory

I love Me, I love my luxuriant Body, not slender

I love me, I love my inside, not concerned how you see me on the outside

I love me, I love my head to my feet, not discreet, 'cause I'm God's creation he made me Perfectly Complete.

Ezekiel 28:12 NIV

I Will Not

I will not change my Ebony Skin

I will not change my Brown Eyes

I will not change my Full Lips

I will not change my Thick Thighs

I will not change my Curvy Hips

I will not change my Thick Size

I will not change my Curly Hair

I will not change my Derrière, and some of us, it's a lot back there

I will thank God for the best Creation in his image, read Genesis.

Genesis 1:27 NIV

Loving Me

Loving me is a must

Loving me is required

Loving me is essential

Loving me is desired

Loving me is significant

Loving me is preferred

Loving me is expected

Loving me is deserved

Loving me is necessary

"Love your neighbor as yourself"

God said it first, if I don't love myself, I can't love anyone else.

Mark 12:31 NIV

Proud

Proud to be Me

Despite my Father

Proud to be me

Despite my Color

Proud to be Me

Despite my Hair

Proud to be Me

Despite my Lips

Proud to be Me

Despite my Hips

Proud to be Me

Despite my Body

Proud to be Me

Despite nothing at all!

Instilled by my mother

I was made in the image of God!

Genesis 1:27 NIV

Self-Esteem High

Been brown since Infancy

Skin melanated like I'm from Egypt see

The many shades of Ebony

Mesmerized 'cause you don't look like me

The world filled with such Jealousy

Head held tall as the sky, out of your reach see

I Know my worth, self-esteem high

Created in God's own image Genesis tells me why.

Genesis 1:27 NIV

I Know my Worth

Precious Gem

My skin glows

Like a Diamond in the night

My skin glows

Like a Sapphire in Sunlight

My skin glows

Like a Topaz in the Sea

My skin glows

Like a Ruby in a Tea Tree

My skin glows

Like Sun-Kissed Amethyst

My skin glows

Like an Alexandrite, so bright, you can't miss it

My skin glows

Like an Emerald over the Rainbow

"I will shine among them like stars in the sky," God said that in

Philippians that's no lie.

Philippians 2:15 NIV

Beauty

Beauty is you

Beauty is me

Beauty is my big smile

Beauty is my white teeth

Beauty is you

Beauty is me

Beauty is my brown eyes

Beauty is my curly hair see

Beauty is you

Beauty is me

Beauty is my wide nose

Beauty is my cheek bones

Beauty is you

Beauty is me

Beauty is my big forehead

Beauty is my full figure

"I am all together beautiful, there is no flaw in me", singing Song of Songs, God

scripture grounds me.

Song of Songs 4:7 NIV

Blessed

Blessed from my head to my feet

Blessed with every heartbeat

Blessed with this oh so thick hair

Blessed with my round Derrière

Blessed with these wide hips

Blessed with these big lips

Blessed with my mile-long legs

Blessed with my brown gorgeous face

Blessed with my nose that's so different

'Cause of the grace, God gave me, it's sufficient.

2 Corinthians 12:9 NIV

Dark Skin

Dark skin girl, skin so soft, skin so lovely

What you not going to do is make me think I'm ugly

Dark skin girl, skin so soft, skin so lovely

I get it from my Daddy he defines me as a Beauty

Dark skin girl, skin so soft, skin so lovely

My smile, so Divine you wonder why I shine

Dark skin girl, skin so soft, skin so lovely

Ebony, Chocolate, Mocha, Caramel and Toffee

Dark skin girl, skin so soft, skin so lovely

I have no shame and yes, my Momma's to blame

Dark skin girl, skin so soft skin so lovely

Created by God and yes, he said he'll always love me.

Psalms 136:26 NIV

Many Shades

The many shades of black, gold & brown

I am fabulous 'cause everybody ain't made this round

The many shades of black, gold & brown

I am fabulous 'cause I make all heads turn when I come around

The many shades of black, gold & brown

I am fabulous 'cause my color is like no other, and oh yeah, I get it from my Mother

The many shades of black, gold & brown

I am fabulous 'cause I demand respect and I won't tolerate anything less

The many shades of black gold & brown

I am fabulous 'cause my God made me this way.

Genesis 1:27 NIV

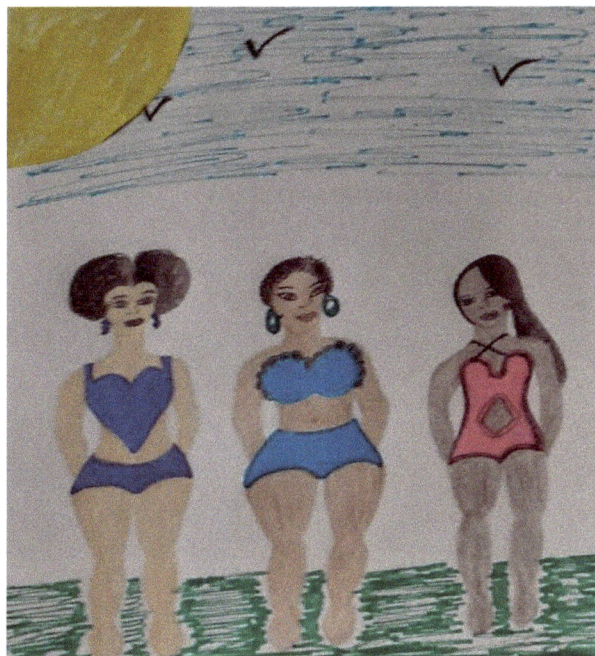

I am

I am Royal

Open your eyes and see me

I am Noble

Open your eyes and see me

I am Sovereign

Open your eyes and see me

I am Magnificent

Open your eyes and see me

I am Exquisite

Open your eyes and see me

I am Majestic

Open your eyes and see me

I am Queen

My God says take pride in my high position, and oh yeah, I see me.

James 1:9 NIV

Royal Love

Love between a King and Queen is everything, I was created specifically for a King

Love between a King and Queen is everything, too powerful to get in-between

Love between a King and Queen is everything, ruling their empire nurtured by the Queen

Love between a King and Queen is everything, protecting each other's hearts from a broken presence in society

Love between a King and Queen is everything, never giving up, never losing faith, always hopeful, no room for negativity

Love between a King and Queen is everything, God explains how a man leaves his parents and is united to his wife and become one physicality.

1 Corinthians 13:7 NIV
Genesis 2:24 NIV

Enough

I can't say I love me enough

When I look in the mirror what do I see,

My beautiful soul looking at me

I can't say I love me enough

When I look in the mirror what do I see,

My self-esteem higher than the sun in the month of June as it sets, see

I can't say I love me enough

When I look in the mirror what do I see

My Triumphs over the probability

I can't say I love me enough

When I look in the mirror what do I see,

My Natural Black features, & Oh that Melanin, you see

I can't say I love me enough

When I look in the mirror what do I see,

God's Property, he lives in me!

1 JOHN 3:24

Self-Worth

Black Girls

Black girls are Courageous

We will not lose

Black girls are Bold

We will never be quiet

Black girls are Intelligent

We have no limits

Black girls are Purposeful

We will advance

Black girls are Enchanting

We have no flaws

Black girls are Extraordinary

We will never be Ordinary

My god says if you believe, you will receive whatever you ask for in prayer.

Matthew 21:22

They Say

They say you don't talk Black

I'm Educated
That's Black Excellence

They say you're not like Black people

I'm Black
That's Black Power

They say you don't act Black

I'm Royalty
That's Black Culture

They say you don't look black

I'm Melanated
That's Black Beauty

You have now been informed of what Black is

God says walk with the Wise and become wise.

Proverbs 13:20

My Color

My Color may not be your favorite, but it sure is mine,

It's the reason I'm Enchanting

My Color may not be your favorite, but it sure is mine,

It's the reason I'm Gorgeous

My Color may not be your favorite, but it sure is mine,

It's the reason I'm Glamorous

My Color may not be your favorite, but it sure is mine.

It's the reason I'm alluring

God said, "be skilled in your art", sounds like you need my color to complete it.

Exodus 35:10

Black Queen

I'm a Black Queen, whose biggest fan is me,

Never ashamed of who I am or who I used to be

I'm a Black Queen whose biggest fan is me,

Never jeopardize my family and I protect them wholeheartedly

I'm a Black Queen whose biggest fan is me,

Never mediocre 'cause someone is always watching me

I'm a Black Queen whose biggest fan is me,

Never weak, stronger than spider silk and will always stay on my feet

I'm a Black Queen whose biggest fan is me,

Never doubt my faith in God he's never doubted me.

Mark 11:22-25

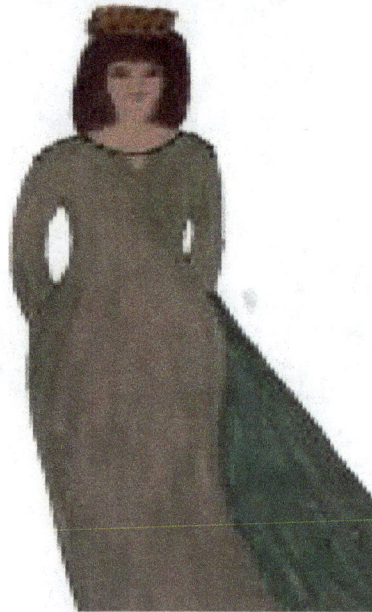

Queen

I'm a Black Queen, I know my position

You can find me on my throne

I'm a Black Queen, I know my position

You see my beauty is that of a Goddess

I'm a Black Queen, I know my position

You see I will never bow down to anyone

I'm a Black Queen, I know my position

You see my heart is that of a Soldier

I'm a Black Queen, I know my position

You see I will never abdicate my throne

"God says your throne will be established forever".

2 Samuel 7:16

Skin tone

My Mocha skin tone is a reflection, of all this perfection

My Mocha skin tone is a reflection, of a diamond, so I stay polished

My mocha skin tone is a reflection, of all this magic, even if you know my next trick

My mocha skin tone is a reflection, of a Star, so I stay Shining

My Mocha skin tone is a reflection, of all this affection

My mocha skin tone is a reflection, of a God so good, that I am fearfully and wonderfully made.

Psalm 139:14

In love with Me

I'm so in love, with me, 'cause I'm a passport to my uncontrollable Destiny

I'm so in love, with me, 'cause I'm a passport to my black girls watching me

I'm so in love, with me, 'cause I'm a passport to my family leaving behind a legacy

I'm so in love with me, 'cause I'm a passport to the throne that entitles me as Queen

I'm so in love with me, 'cause I'm a passport to Black girls that look like me

I'm so in love with me, 'cause I'm a passport to success after failing repeatedly

I'm so in love with me, 'cause I'm a defined testimony of who God says I should be.

1 John 5:9

Thick Brown Hair

Ooh Wee, my thick brown hair gives me such peace, knowing everybody can't use my grease

Ooh Wee, my thick brown hair gives me such peace, the bigger it is the more they glare at me

Ooh Wee, my thick brown hair gives me such peace, it grows up and out like a crown, that's the Queen in me

Ooh Wee, my thick brown hair gives me such peace, Afro so heavenly, that's the Angel in me.

Ooh Wee, my thick brown hair gives me such peace, so kinky, so curly, so locked, that's what's up.

Ooh wee, my thick brown hair gives me such peace, Please, understand God created me.

Genesis 1:27 NIV

My Grin

Ear to Ear, you see my grin, that's 'cause I'm pleased with the skin I'm in, black like tourmaline, full of energy that's me

Ear to Ear, you see my grin, that's 'cause I'm pleased with the thick hair on my head, dark like Onyx, protecting what's mines

Ear to Ear you see my grin, that's 'cause I'm pleased with the fullness of my lips, plump like cherries, stunning and magnificent

Ear to Ear you see my grin, that's 'cause I'm pleased with my eye-catching derrière, round like a Diamond, yeah you see it over here

Ear to Ear you see my grin, that's 'cause I'm pleased with my God, he said, "May the righteous be glad and rejoice in him; be happy and joyful".

Psalms 68:3 NIV

Respect

I respect me, so just know, once you overstep your boundary, it's a wrap with me

I respect me, so just know, I don't have to reveal my body, for you to see my Beauty, you see

I respect me, so just know, if you are intimidated by my Posture, that's your own insecurities

I respect me, so just know, my protection as a black girl is a top priority, to me

I respect me so just know, my God said, "Whoever respects a command is rewarded," that's me.

Proverbs 13:13 NIV

Creativity

My creativity amazes me, from my heartbeat to the rhythm of my soulful feet

My creativity amazes me, passed down from my ancestors, no wonder why you always copying me

My creativity amazes me, my style, my brilliance, my finesse is unmatched, can't you see

My creativity amazes me, no matter how small my creation, it's an abundant sensation

My creativity amazes me, for I am God's handiwork, created to do good works which he prepared just for me.

Ephesians 2:10 NIV

I Validate Me

I am my own validation see, 'cause once you stop believing in me, I will still achieve

I am my own validation see, 'cause once you start condemning me, best believe I will triumph, you hear me

I am my own validation see, 'cause once I departed from the womb, I was raised by a black woman who set the standard for me

I am my own validation see, 'cause once you find out my lane has expanded further than yours, you get a little envious of me

I am my own validation see, 'cause once I pray to my God, he will sustain me and never let me be shaken.

Psalms 55:22 NIV

Mother

My Mother is mine all mine; she's a refined Queen of her Throne, she can never be replaced

My mother is mine all mine; she's a refined Queen of her Throne, see, she nurture's the masses, planting seeds along the way

My mother is mine all mine; she's a refined Queen of her Throne, designed as a masterpiece

My mother is mine all mine; she's a refined Queen of her Throne, in position to protect us from any calamity

My mother is mine all mine; she's a refined Queen of her Throne, which God says is established through righteousness.

Proverbs 16:12 NIV

Black Love

Black love, a love so forceful it leaves you confused

Black love, a love so unbreakable even bullets can't pass through

Black love, a love so resistant you can't intercede

Black love, a love so heavy only the person it's meant for can carry

Black love, a love so extreme, it gets deep down in your spirit, you know what I mean

Black love, God said, "Be devoted to one another in love, honor one another above yourselves".

Romans 12:10 NIV

Girl of Color

I love me for who I am, who I was and who I used to be, still a girl of color, I know you're not looking for an apology

I love me for who I am, who I was and who I used to be, still a girl of color, delighted to be me

I love me for who I am, who I was and who I used to be, still a girl of color, I see you looking at me with such envy, I'm just being me

I love me for who I am, who I was and who I used to be, still a girl of color, all the power is possessed in me, I'll be who I want to be

I love me for who I am, who I was and who I used to be, still a girl of color, "Praise be to God, who has not rejected my prayer or withheld his love from me"!

Psalms 66:20 NIV

Self-Esteem High

Know your Worth

I glitter like Gold

I am pure and rare like Platinum

Radiant as a Pearl

Know your worth little black girl

I won't take no for an answer

I won't accept your excuses

I won't conform to your world

Know your worth little black girl

I am Persistent

I am Brave

I am Responsible

Know your worth little black girl

I won't Fail

I won't Lose

I won't Let you down

Know your worth little black girl

I am Divine

I am Passionate

I am Impressive

Know your worth little black girl

I can do all things because my God gives me Strength. Philippians 4:13

Beauty is Me

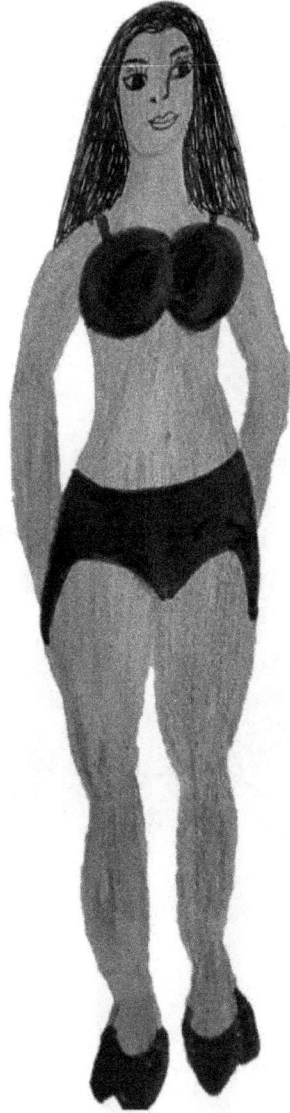

References

The New International Version of the Holy Bible

Genesis 1:27
So, God created mankind in his own image, in the image of God he created them; male and female he created them.

Philippians 2:15
And pure, children of God without fault in a warped and crooked generation. Then you will shine among them like stars in the sky.

1 Peter 3:5
Rather, it should be that of your inner self, the unfading beauty of a gentle and quiet spirit, which is of great worth in God's sight.

Ephesians 4:29
Do not let any unwholesome talk come out of your mouths, but only what is helpful for building others up according to their needs, that it may benefit those who listen.

Ezekiel 28:12
You were the seal of perfection, full of wisdom and perfect in beauty.

Psalm 139 13-14
For you created my inmost being you knit me together in my mother's womb. I praise you because I am fearfully and wonderfully made; your works are wonderful; I know that full well.

Mark 12:31
The second is this: "Love your neighbor as yourself". There is no commandment greater than these.

Song of Songs 4:7
You are altogether beautiful, my darling; there is no flaw in you.

2 Corinthians 12:9
But he said to me, "My grace is sufficient for you, for my power is made perfect in weakness". Therefore, I will boast even more gladly about my weaknesses, so that Christ's power may rest on me.

Psalms 136:26
Give thanks to the God of heaven. His love endures forever.

James 1:9
Believers in humble circumstances ought to take pride in their high position.

1 Corinthians 13:7
It always protects, always trusts, always hopes, always perseveres.

Genesis 2:24
That is why a man leaves his father and mother and is united to his wife, and they become one flesh.

I John 3:24
The one that keeps God's commands lives in him, and he in them. And this is how we know that he lives in us: We know it by the Spirit he gave us.

Matthew 21:22
"If you believe, you will receive whatever you ask for in prayer."

Proverbs 13:20
Walk with the wise and become wise, for a companion of fools suffer harm.

Exodus 35:10
All who are skilled among you are to come and make everything the lord has commanded.

Mark 11:22-25
"Have faith in God," Jesus answered. "Truly I tell you, if anyone says to this mountain, Go, throw yourself into the sea. And does not doubt in their heart but believes that what they say will happen; it will be done for them."

2 Samuel 7:16
"Your house and your Kingdom will endure forever before me; your throne will be established forever."

Exodus 35:10
All who are skilled among you are to come and make everything the lord has commanded.

Mark 11:22-25
"Have faith in God," Jesus answered. "Truly I tell you, if anyone says to this mountain, Go, throw yourself into the sea. And does not doubt in their heart but believes that what they say will happen; it will be done for them."

2 Samuel 7:16
"Your house and your Kingdom will endure forever before me; your throne will be established forever."

1 John 5:9
We accept human testimony, but God's testimony is greater because it is the testimony of God, which he has given about his son.

Psalm 68:3
But may the righteous be glad and rejoice before God; may they be happy and joyful.

Proverbs 13:13
Whoever scorns instruction will pay for it, but whoever respects a command is rewarded.

Ephesians 2:10
For we are God's handiwork, created in Christ Jesus to do good works, which God prepared in advance for us to do.

Psalms 55:22
Cast your cares on the Lord and he will sustain you; he will never let the righteous be shaken.

Proverbs 16:12
Kings detest wrongdoing, for a throne is established through righteousness.

Romans 12:10
Be devoted to one another in love. Honor one another above yourselves.

Psalm 66:20
Praise be to God, who has not rejected my prayer or withheld his love from me!

1 Corinthians 13:7
It always protects, always trusts, always hopes, always perseveres.

Philippians 4:13
I can do all things through him who gives me strength.
That is why a man leaves his father and mother and is united to his wife, and
they become one flesh.